Philippines
the culture

Greg Nickles

A Bobbie Kalman Book

The Lands, Peoples, and Cultures Series

Crabtree Publishing Company
www.crabtreebooks.com

The Lands, Peoples, and Cultures Series

Created by Bobbie Kalman

Coordinating editor
Ellen Rodger

Project editor
Carrie Gleason

Production coordinator
Rosie Gowsell

Project development, photo research, and design
First Folio Resource Group, Inc.
  Erinn Banting
  Tom Dart
  Söğüt Y. Güleç
  Alana Lai
  Debbie Smith

Editing
Carolyn Black

Prepress and Printing
Worzalla Publishing Company

Consultants
Maria Genitrix P. Nañes, Philippine Consulate General (Toronto)

Photographs
Corbis/Magma Photo News Inc./AFP: p. 8 (left), p. 10 (right), p. 13 (bottom), p. 21 (bottom); Corbis/Magma Photo News Inc./Paul Almasy: p. 22 (left), p. 29 (right); Corbis/Magma Photo News Inc./Bettmann: p. 29 (left); Corbis/Magma Photo News Inc./Jan Butchofsky-Houser: p. 20; Corbis/Magma Photo News Inc./Dean Conger: p. 22 (right), p. 23 (left); Corbis/Magma Photo News Inc./Bennett Dean: p. 19 (top); Corbis/Magma Photo News Inc./Leonard de Selva: p. 28; Corbis/Magma Photo News Inc./Gacad; Romeo: p. 13 (top); Corbis/Magma Photo News Inc./Robert Holmes: p. 23 (right); Corbis/Magma Photo News Inc./Catherine Karnow: p. 9 (bottom); Corbis/Magma Photo News Inc./Paul A. Souders: p. 9 (top), p. 11, p. 18, p. 24 (both); Stuart Dee: cover; Mark Downey/Lucid

Images: title page, p. 4, p. 5 (both), p. 6 (top), p. 7, p. 12 (left), p. 14 (right), p. 25; Alain Evrard/Photo Researchers: p. 14 (left); Aaron Favila/Associated Press/AP: p. 17 (bottom); Veronica Garbuti/Panos Pictures: p. 10 (left); Oliver Garcia/Panos Pictures: p. 19 (bottom); Jay Ireland & Georgienne E. Bradley/Bradleyireland.com: p. 26; Robin Laurance/Photo Researchers: p. 12 (right); Edwin Leynes: p. 16 (bottom); Bullit Marquez/Associated Press/AP: p. 16 (top); Pat Roque/Associated Press/AP: p. 17 (top); Blair Seitz/Photo Researchers: title page, p. 3; Sean Sprague/Panos Pictures: p. 15; Chris Stowers/Panos Pictures: p. 27; Flora Torrance/Life File: p. 6 (bottom), p. 8 (right), p. 21 (top)

Illustrations
Diane Eastman: icon
Carolyn Platon-Villasanta: pp. 30–31
David Wysotski, Allure Illustrations: back cover

Cover: The sails of this traditional ferryboat, called a *vinta*, are woven from brightly colored fabric. Weaving is a prized skill in the Philippines.

Title page: People dress up in colorful costumes during *Dinagyang*, a festival that honors Jesus Christ.

Icon: A panpipe, which is an instrument made from several pipes tied together, appears at the head of each section.

Back cover: Pangolins are covered in hard scales. When they are threatened, they roll into a ball and use their scales to defend themselves.

Published by
Crabtree Publishing Company

PMB 16A,
350 Fifth Avenue
Suite 3308
New York
N.Y. 10118

612 Welland Avenue
St. Catharines
Ontario, Canada
L2M 5V6

73 Lime Walk
Headington
Oxford OX3 7AD
United Kingdom

Cataloging in Publication Data

Nickles, Greg, 1969-
    Philippines. The culture / Greg Nickles.
       p. cm. -- (The lands, peoples, and cultures series)
    Includes index.
    Summary: Introduces the different religions, festivals, arts and music, languages, and literature that are part of the Filipino culture.
       ISBN 0-7787-9354-0 (RLB) -- ISBN 0-7787-9722-8 (pbk.)
       1. Philippines--Civilization--Juvenile literature. [1. Philippines--Civilization.] I. Title. II. Series.
DS664 .N53 2002
959.9--dc21   2001047111
                                                              LC

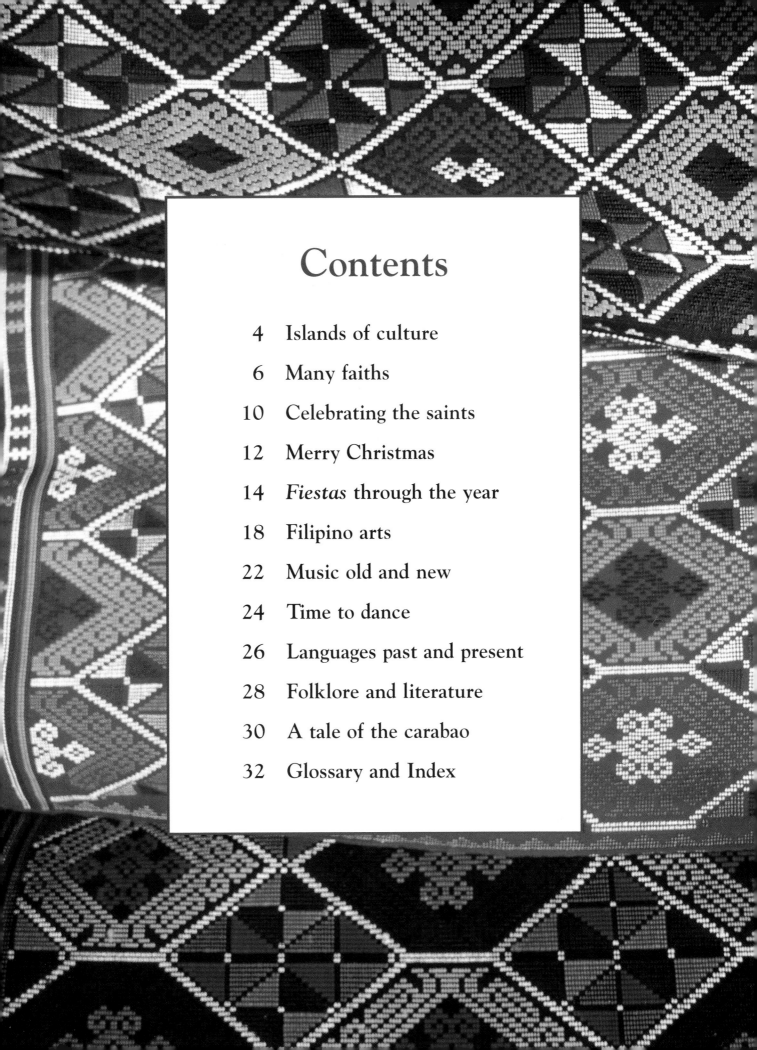

Contents

Islands of culture

The culture of the Philippines is very rich in legends and folktales. According to one tale, long ago the world was filled with plants and animals, but no people. One day, the mighty King of the Birds was exploring the world. Tired of flying, he landed on a tall, fat stalk of **bamboo** to rest. He was surprised to hear muffled voices from inside. "Free us, please!" called the voices.

The mighty bird split the bamboo open with a single peck of his beak. From inside sprang a man and woman.

The King of the Birds admired their beauty. "Climb onto my back, and we shall fly the world together," he offered. "The most beautiful place we see shall become your homeland."

The man and woman held on tightly as the mighty bird soared through the skies in search of their new home. At last, they came to a group of islands that were as beautiful and green as emeralds. The King of the Birds landed and the people hopped from his back. These islands, the Philippines, became their home. The man and the woman, Malakas and Maganda, were the first two Filipinos, or people of the Philippines.

The Filipinos

Today, about 70 different groups of Filipino peoples make their home on the islands. Each group speaks its own language and practices its own mix of ancient and modern **customs**. The culture of the Philippines combines all these customs, arts, styles of music, and languages.

Culture from around the world

People from other countries have had a strong influence on Filipino culture. In the 1500s, Spain conquered the Philippines and ruled for more than 300 years. They introduced Filipinos to many of their traditions, including their religion — Christianity. Then, in 1898, the United States bought the Philippines from Spain and ruled until the Philippines became an independent country in 1946. Elements of their culture also became part of Filipinos' everyday lives, including the English language.

A musician from the southern island of Mindanao plays a gong by hitting it with a stick. Gongs of different sizes are played at special occasions and festivals throughout the Philippines.

Children gather in front of the Betis Church in Pampanga, on the northern island of Luzon. The intricate carvings and decorations on the church, which was built in the 1700s, reflect the Spanish influence on Filipino architecture.

The Maria Clara Suite is a traditional style of Spanish dance that is popular in the Philippines. Filipinos have added their own touches to these dances, using bamboo castanets and special fans called **abanicos***.*

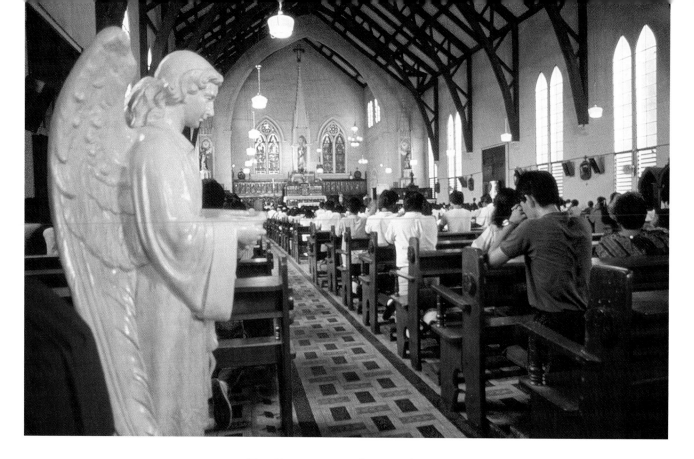

Many faiths

Most Filipinos hold strong religious beliefs. They regularly take part in religious ceremonies and celebrate holy days with large festivals. The majority of Filipinos practice the Christian religion. The religion of Islam has the second largest following. Some Filipinos are **animists**, which means that they worship the spirits of plants, animals, and other objects in nature.

What is Christianity?

Christianity is a religion based on the teachings of Jesus Christ, whom Christians believe is the son of God. About 85 percent of Filipinos belong to the Roman Catholic Church. Roman Catholicism is a **denomination** of Christianity that the Spanish introduced to the Philippines in the 1500s. The high number of Christians in the Philippines today makes it one of the largest Christian countries in the world. It is also the only Asian country where Christianity is the main religion.

(top) Roman Catholic worshipers pray during a service at St. Paul's Cathedral in Manila, on Luzon.

The Baclayon Church, on Bohol, was built in 1595. It is one of the oldest churches in the Philippines.

Part of daily life

Roman Catholic beliefs play an important part in the daily lives of most Filipinos. Worshipers honor Christ; his mother, Mary; and other **holy** people called **saints**. Filipinos look to these holy people for help and protection. Many Filipinos decorate their homes, schools, buses, and ferryboats with images of Christ, Mary, and the saints. They also name rivers, streets, villages, and other landmarks throughout the country in honor of them.

Roman Catholic priests, or men who devote their lives to God, play a large role in daily life. They perform weddings, **baptize** babies, lead religious ceremonies, and offer advice to people in their community.

Other Christians

Aglipayans are members of the Philippine Independent Church. Two Filipinos, Gregorio Aglipay and Isabelo de los Reyes, founded this Christian denomination in 1902. Both Aglipay and de los Reyes worked with Filipinos in the late 1800s to free the land from Spanish control. Their Philippine Independent Church attracted many followers because, unlike the local Roman Catholic Church at the time, it was run by Filipinos instead of the Spanish.

The strict *Iglesia ni Kristo*, or Church of Christ, is another Christian denomination in the Philippines. The church was founded in 1914 by Felix Manalo, who followers believe was a **prophet**.

Throughout the Philippines, people set up outdoor shrines where they honor and pray to saints. Two nuns, or women who devote their lives to God, leave a shrine dedicated to Jesus' mother, Mary, on the island of Panay.

The legend of Abu Bakkar

The Tausug are a group of Muslim peoples who live in the southern part of the Philippines. They became Muslim after a legendary Muslim adventurer named Abu Bakkar came to their territory in the mid-1400s. He married into the royal family, inherited the kingdom, became the ruler, and declared Islam the religion of the Tausug.

(above) Three girls wearing traditional Muslim head coverings wait for the beginning of a prayer service at a mosque, or Muslim place of worship, in Manila.

Muslim Filipinos

Traders and **missionaries** from nearby islands and China introduced Islam to Filipinos in the 1200s. Today, several million Muslims live in the Philippines, mainly on the southern islands. Muslims follow the religion of Islam, which is based on the holy book called the *Qur'an*. The *Qur'an* contains the teachings and instructions of God, whom Muslims call *Allah*. Religious officials in Muslim communities include the *imam*, who leads people in prayer; the *kadi*, or judge; and the *hatib*, who delivers sermons.

Some Filipinos practice Taoism, which is a religious belief that originated in China. The biggest Taoist temple in the Philippines is in Cebu City, on the central island of Cebu.

Traditional beliefs

Long before Christianity and Islam came to the Philippines, people on the islands were animists. Today, some Filipinos, especially in the countryside, are still animists. They believe in gods and spirits who control disease, the weather, the sun, the moon, and the sky. Animists perform special ceremonies to keep these gods and spirits happy, such as offering them food and gifts.

Animists also believe that people, animals, plants, and other natural objects have spirits. Many think that a person's spirit leaves his or her body during sleep or illness. If an evil force captures the spirit while it is away from the body, the person dies.

Healers and priests

In many Filipino communities, especially in rural areas, healers and priests lead ceremonies based on ancient animist beliefs. Some ceremonies mark the birth of a baby, a wedding, or a funeral. Other ceremonies are performed to cure diseases or predict the future.

Ifugao gods and spirits

The Ifugao people live on the northern island of Luzon. They believe in about 1,500 gods or spirits. Ifugao priests know all these gods and spirits by name, and perform special ceremonies to communicate with them. Sometimes, up to fifteen priests perform these ceremonies together. People believe that while the priests chant and pray, spirits enter their bodies. The priests then eat offerings of food and drink to please the spirits.

One pesky Ifugao spirit is the *halupe*. A *halupe* can interrupt someone's thoughts and may be sent by one Ifugao to control another's actions. For example, a *halupe* might remind someone again and again to repay a debt.

Some people believe that faith healers can cure diseases that usually require surgery by passing their hands over the part of the body that is diseased.

(above) At a funeral on Luzon, an Ifugao man cooks the head of a pig that was sacrificed as an offering to the gods. The skull of the pig will then be hung outside the home of the deceased's family to protect family members from evil spirits.

Roman Catholic Filipinos worship and celebrate saints in many ways. Like Roman Catholics around the world, they believe that a different saint protects each profession, village, town, and city. Each saint, known as a patron saint, is honored on a particular day of the year. When the day arrives, people hold a big *fiesta*, or festival, with parades, music, dancing, feasting, and games.

Holy parades

One of the main celebrations at a saint's day is a **procession**, during which people carry a painting or sculpture of their patron saint through the streets. The paintings or sculptures usually stand on *andas*, which are decorated platforms that people carry on their shoulders. Sometimes, the paintings or sculptures roll down the streets on *carrozas*, larger platforms with wheels. Worshipers follow the images, holding lighted candles and chanting or singing.

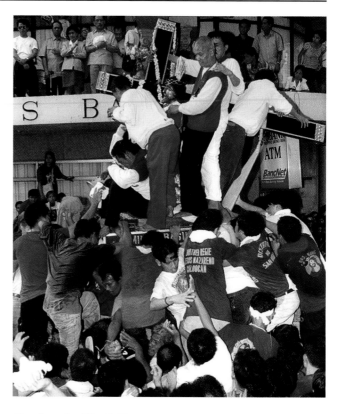

During the Black Nazarene Procession, people who wish to be healed climb to the top of the statue of Christ while it is carried through the streets.

The Black Nazarene Procession

The largest procession in the Philippines is the Black Nazarene Procession, held on January 9 in Quiapo, on the island of Luzon. A black, wooden sculpture of Christ, Quiapo's patron saint, is beautifully decorated in rich fabrics and pulled through the streets on a cart. The Spanish brought this sculpture to the town from Europe in the 1500s. More than a hundred thousand people come each year to take part in the procession. Many of them try to touch the statue, hoping that Christ will bless them, heal their illnesses, or help with other troubles.

*People crowd around an **andas** carrying a statue of Mary, during the **Turumba** Festival in Pakil, on Luzon. The festival was named "turumba," which means "singing and dancing," because that was how the original participants celebrated their patron saint.*

Santacruzan

In May, villages, towns, and cities in many parts of the Philippines celebrate *Santacruzan*, a *fiesta* that honors Saint Helen. It is believed that in 326 A.D., Saint Helen discovered the cross on which Christ was **crucified**, in Jerusalem, in present-day Israel. A major part of some *Santacruzan* celebrations is a reenactment of Saint Helen's discovery. A young girl dresses up as Helen, while a young boy plays her son, the Roman ruler Constantine. People gather in the town square to watch the girl and boy, accompanied by other children, dig up mounds of earth in search of the cross. At the third mound, the girl finds a small wooden cross — which represents Christ's cross — and holds it up with a cheer. Then, the feasting and music begin.

Carabao festivals

On May 14, many Filipino farmers honor their patron saint, Saint Isidro Labrador. He was a humble, hard-working Spanish farmer, who used a team of oxen to plow his land. One day, after returning home from prayer, he discovered that a miracle had happened — an angel had finished his work in the fields! God had rewarded him for his hard work and devotion.

Many people use Saint Isidro Labrador's day to celebrate their carabao, the gentle, sturdy water buffalo that helps with their farmwork. On the morning of the holiday, families wash their carabao, polish its hooves, and decorate it with colorful fabrics, flowers, and ribbons. Some shave patterns into their carabao's fur. They put an image of Saint Isidro Labrador, along with fruit and farming tools, on their cart. After harnessing their carabao to the cart, the families ride to church. There, the priest blesses the animals during **mass**. Later, families enter their carabao in races, strength and beauty contests, and other fun competitions.

People with painted faces and large, elaborate masks are a common sight at the **Ati-Atihan** *festival in Kalibo, on Panay.*

Ati-Atihan

People in the town of Kalibo, on the island of Panay, celebrate *Ati-Atihan* on the third weekend in January. This festival honors the island's patron saint Santo Niño, Christ Child. It also celebrates the people of Kalibo's friendship with the Ati, who live in the nearby mountains. A legend tells of a terrible rainfall that ruined the Ati's crops in the 1200s. When the Ati came to Kalibo in search of food, the townspeople offered to share their rice crops with them. The two peoples have been friends ever since.

Ati-Atihan is an exciting festival with music, dance, costumes, and masks. The Ati join the people of Kalibo in the celebration. With soot covering their bodies and large hats decorated with feathers and beads on their heads, both groups blow whistles and bang drums, pots, and pans. After a mass at the end of the festival, people bathe in the river to get the soot off.

On Christmas, or *Pasko* as it is called in the Philippines, Christians celebrate the birth of Jesus Christ. Christmas Day is on December 25, but the celebrations start several weeks earlier as Filipinos begin to wish one another *"Maligayang Pasko"* or "Merry Christmas."

Beginning the *fiesta*

Pasko starts officially on the morning of December 16. Bells, Christmas carols, and fireworks awaken people at four o'clock in the morning, so they can go to church. The early mass they attend is called *Misa de Gallo*, or "Mass of the Rooster," because it happens right before sunrise, when roosters crow. After mass, families stop at food stalls in the churchyard for Christmas treats such as hot ginger tea or *bibingka*, a rice-flour pancake cooked on banana leaves.

Preparing the home

For the next eight mornings, people rise early for *Misa de Gallo*. During this time, they decorate their home for the main *Pasko* celebrations. They clean, prepare delicious holiday food, and either buy a Christmas tree or make one from branches, palm leaves, or cardboard. Families also set up *belens*, or Nativity scenes, showing the different people who were at the stable where Jesus Christ was born. The figure of the baby Jesus is not added to the scene until Christmas Day.

(above) **Bibingka** *are made with mochi rice and coconuts, and are cooked on banana leaves.*

(right) A craftsperson carefully weaves palm branches together into sections. Then, she ties the sections together and trims them to look like a Christmas tree.

Brightly colored **parol** *decorate the front of a booth at an outdoor market in Manila.*

Shining stars

A special Filipino Christmas decoration is the *parol*. A *parol* is a star made from a bamboo frame covered with rice paper. A candle or light is placed inside of it to make it glow. These bright stars hang in windows everywhere. They remind people of the star that appeared in the sky when Christ was born.

Noche Buena

On Christmas Eve, the night of December 24, people go to church for a late mass which is sometimes held at midnight. Afterward, many families return home for a huge feast called *Noche Buena*, or "Good Night." *Noche Buena* lasts into the early hours of the morning. The meal features special dishes such as *arroz caldo*, a chicken soup with rice; *lumpia*, which are spring rolls stuffed with meat or vegetables; and a lot of meat, including chicken stuffed with pork and sausages. Traditional desserts include *bibingka* and *calamay*, a sweet rice pudding served in a coconut shell. For children, the highlight of *Noche Buena* is when they receive Christmas gifts from their parents and grandparents.

Ending the season

Pasko ends with the Feast of the Three Kings, which usually takes place on the first Sunday in January. On this day, people remember the three kings who brought gifts to Jesus when he was born. The night before the Feast of the Three Kings, children leave their shoes by a window when they go to bed. They hope that the kings will come during the night and place a gift inside their shoes. In church the next day, people reenact the kings' search for the baby Jesus.

Smiling children show off the gifts they found in their shoes on the morning of the Feast of the Three Kings.

13

On the island of Marinduque, south of Luzon, performers present one of the most elaborate plays at the *Moriones*, or "Masks," Festival. Actors wear frightening masks, pretending to be the Roman soldiers who crucified Christ. They perform the story of Longinus, a soldier who was blind in one eye. Longinus helped in the crucifixion by stabbing Christ in the side with his **lance**. When a drop of Christ's blood fell into Longinus's eye, a miracle happened. Longinus was able to see again! Immediately, Longinus became a believer in Christ and his powers. This angered the other Roman soldiers, who killed Longinus.

People in Pahiyas, on the island of Quezon, begin decorating their homes and shops on May 1 to get ready for their harvest festival on May 15.

Besides saints' days and Christmas, Filipinos celebrate many other *fiestas*. Some are religious, such as Christian or Muslim celebrations, while others are national holidays, such as Independence Day on June 12. Many other *fiestas* mark seasonal events, such as the end of the harvest.

The *Moriones* Festival

During Easter, which takes place in March or April, Christians remember Christ's death and resurrection, or return to life. Filipinos attend church services, walk in processions, and watch long plays that tell the story of Christ's life.

*A young boy holds a colorful mask of a Roman soldier. It is part of his costume for the **Moriones** Festival.*

Flores de Mayo

Flores de Mayo, or "Flowers of May," lasts throughout the month of May. It is connected to *Santacruzan*. Each day, girls crowned with wreaths of flowers and dressed in white gowns walk in a procession to church. There, they pray, sing, and lay their wreaths in front of an image of Christ's mother, Mary. If enough girls live in a community, a different group performs this ceremony each day of the festival. The celebration ends with a feast on the last Sunday of May.

Ramadan

Ramadan is a holy time of year for Muslims around the world. It is the ninth month of the Muslim calendar. Muslims believe that, during *Ramadan*, the prophet Muhammad first received *Allah*'s teachings. As he taught *Allah*'s messages to others, Islam spread throughout the world.

During the entire month of *Ramadan*, adults and many older children **fast** from sunrise to sunset. They believe the fast teaches them self-discipline, cleanses their spirit, and helps them understand how the poor and hungry feel. They break their fast at the end of each day with a meal called *iftar*.

Muslims pray five times a day: before sunrise, in early afternoon, in late afternoon, after sunset, and before going to bed. During Ramadan, they say extra nightly prayers called **taraweeh***.*

The day after *Ramadan* ends, Muslim Filipinos celebrate *Hari Raya Puasa*. They take an early-morning bath, put on fresh clothes, say special prayers, and visit family. Later, they celebrate with a feast. A special *Hari Raya Puasa* custom involves visiting the graves of loved ones. Like many other Muslims, the Maranao people on the southern island of Mindanao clean their family's graves and light candles at the cemetery at night. They also light candles at home, hoping to glimpse a legendary angel named Lailatol Kadr, whom they say grants wishes.

The Muslim calendar

Holidays such as Christmas and New Year follow the solar year, which is the time it takes the earth to orbit around the sun. The solar year has 365 days, or 366 days during a leap year. The Muslim calendar is based on the lunar year. Each month begins when a new moon appears. The lunar year is approximately eleven days shorter than the solar year, so each year, Muslim holidays such as *Ramadan* start about eleven days earlier than the year before. For example, *Ramadan* may start in the middle of June one year, the beginning of June the next year, and the middle of May the year after that.

In Baguio, on Luzon, people celebrate a flower festival on February 17 with a parade. Participants ride on floats covered in flowers or walk and carry baskets of flowers on their heads.

Ifugao harvest festival

The Ifugao people, who believe in animism, have traditional festivals to celebrate the planting and harvesting of their rice crops. During the harvest, the Ifugao bring out special statues called *bulol*, which represent spirits that protect the rice. The Ifugao believe the *bulol* have supernatural powers. Some say the *bulol* can even leap to safety during a fire!

Higantes festivals

Higantes, or giants, sometimes visit festivals in the Philippines. The giants are actually puppets, up to fourteen feet (four meters) tall, that are made of **papier-mâché**, fabric, and bamboo. Puppeteers, who stand inside the lower part of the *higantes*, use poles to make them dance, bow, and swing their arms. Often, the giants look like farmers or national heroes, such as José Rizal, a doctor and author who spoke out against the Philippines' Spanish rulers in the late 1800s.

Two well-known festivals featuring *higantes* take place on Luzon. Each February, dances and competitions with *higantes* dressed as scarecrows fill the streets of Bayawan, on the island of Negros. These events are part of *Tawo-Tawo*, a festival that honors the *tawo-tawo*, or scarecrows, that protect the crops. Another well-known *higantes* festival takes place in November, when people in the town of Angono, on the island of Luzon, honor San Clemente, the patron saint of fishers. *Higantes* and a brass band follow a procession carrying the saint's image.

*Two girls help their friend into her **higantes** costume before a parade.*

Happy New Year!

Filipinos believe that the first day of the year is a sign of what the rest of the year will be like, so on New Year's Eve and New Year's Day they make sure to do things that they enjoy. Families greet the new year with a special midnight dinner because they hope that they will eat well all year. They wear clothes with polka dots and eat round or oval foods such as eggs because they believe that round objects bring good luck.

The stroke of midnight

Filipinos believe that the noisier the celebration, the better the new year will be, so on New Year's Eve they light fireworks and bang on drums, pots, and pans. Near the stroke of midnight, Filipinos turn on all the lights in their home to welcome in a bright new year. Many attend a special midnight mass or go to church on New Year's Day.

Filipinos of Chinese descent celebrate the Chinese New Year with parades, music, dancing, and a lot of food. The Chinese New Year begins on the first full moon of the new year.

Shoppers buy grapes for their New Year's celebrations. They believe that if they eat twelve grapes as midnight approaches — one grape for each month of the year — they will have good luck.

Filipinos have created beautiful arts and crafts for thousands of years, using materials such as bamboo, wood, paper, and textiles. Artists still do some older folk arts by hand, including woodcarving, metalworking, weaving, and pottery. Other artists explore newer arts, such as painting, photography, and filmmaking.

Wood sculpture

Filipino **artisans** create all kinds of wooden crafts, including household decorations, tools, furniture, and utensils, such as bowls. The Ifugao, who carve animal designs into wooden tools and household objects, are one of several peoples on Luzon known for their woodcarving skills. The Maranao people of Mindanao are also skilled wood sculptors. Special features of Maranao homes are detailed carvings of plants, flowers, birds, and dragons that decorate wooden beams.

This artist is making statues for churches by pouring plaster into molds in the shape of Christian holy people. Other artisans carve the statues out of limestone, a type of rock.

Sculptures of gods and saints

Before the Spanish controlled the Philippines, Filipino carvers created sculptures of their traditional gods. When the Spanish arrived, they encouraged Filipinos to make sculptures of Christian figures, such as Christ, his mother, Mary, and the saints, instead. Today, many of these sculptures stand in churches throughout the country. Some peoples in the countryside still carve statues of traditional gods, such as the Ifugao who create *bulol* to protect granaries.

Weaving

Weaving is one of the most prized skills in the Philippines. Weavers use various materials in their work, including cotton, silk, and even fibers from tree bark and from the leaves of pineapple and banana plants. They make everything from heavy blankets and mats to beautiful, delicate fabrics in bright colors. Some colors are woven into fabrics in complex geometric patterns, while others are tie-dyed. To tie-dye, people tie fabric in knots, then they dip the fabric in dye. After the fabric is dry and the knots are untied, colored patterns are left where the knots once were.

*(left) A craftsperson from Luzon carves a **bulol** using a hammer and chisel.*

(below) Most people in the Philippines still weave fabric on wooden looms. The bright fabric that this woman from Zamboanga, on Mindanao, is weaving will be used to make a blanket.

Metalwork

Metalwork is another specialty of Filipino artisans. Families in the Luzon city of Baguio handcraft delicate jewelry. The T'boli people in the south create ankle and wrist bracelets, and other ornaments which are worn for their beauty, to show off wealth, and to please T'boli gods. The Maranao people make a short dagger called a *sondang* and a long-bladed sword called a *kampilan*, which are part of their traditional costume. Some pieces of metalwork are made from precious metals, such as silver, while others are made out of recycled items such as car parts.

Seashells by the seashore

Filipino artisans use the many seashells found around their islands to make a wide variety of crafts. Shells are used to make jewelry, such as bracelets and earrings, or to decorate jewelry boxes, picture frames, jars, and guitars. Mother-of-pearl, which is the smooth substance that lines the inside of shells, is used to decorate the handles of Maranao *sondang* and *kampilan*.

Lampshades made from thousands of tiny seashells hang at a market on the central island of Mactan.

Painting

Early Filipino painters created intricate designs on pottery and ceramics. Under Spanish rule, Filipino painters began to create Christian artwork, including pictures of saints and scenes from the Bible. Their paintings were done on canvas and walls, especially the walls of churches. Then, in the late 1700s, Filipinos began painting other subjects, such as portraits of important local officials. In the 1800s, Damian Domingo became known for his beautiful, detailed paintings of Filipinos from different backgrounds. His work inspired a new generation of artists, who called him the "father of Filipino painting."

In the 1900s, painters began to depict different subjects in their art. José Joya (1931–1995) created large paintings with brightly colored swirling shapes and lines. Vicente Manansala (1920–1981) and Carlos Francisco (1913–1969) created huge murals on public and private buildings in addition to their paintings on canvas. Manansala's mural on the Medicine Building at the University of Santo Tomas, in Manila, shows the history of medicine in the Philippines. Francisco's murals at the Manila City Hall show scenes from the city's past.

A large mural above a public fountain in Manila shows people helping each other and working together.

Making movies

The Philippines has one of the world's largest movie and television industries. Thousands of movies have been made in the country since José Nepomuceno filmed the first official Filipino movie, *Dalagang Bukid* ("Farm Lass"), in 1919. Many movies, such as the 1977 film *Mababangong Bangungot* ("Perfumed Nightmare"), about a young Filipino in love with American culture, win awards throughout the world. Today, the industry makes an average of 150 films a year. Most are romances, family dramas, comedies, or action-adventures. The Philippines is also a popular place for movie directors from around the world, who film in the country's forests and cities.

In 1998, Filipinos elected one of their movie idols, Joseph Estrada, as president. Estrada, nicknamed "Erap," was famous for his roles as an action hero. Unfortunately, he was soon accused of **corruption**, and Filipinos drove him out of office in 2001.

Cartoons and animation

In addition to films, the Philippines has a large industry devoted to making cartoons. Filipino artists create comic strips and comic books about superheroes and other adventurers. Philippine animation studios also produce television cartoons for large American companies such as Hanna Barbera, and help make movies, such as *The Little Mermaid* and *Beauty and the Beast*, for Disney.

Well-known Filipino sculptor José Abueva and his assistant assemble a monument honoring Jesus Christ in a Manila park.

A **palabunibuniyan**, *or group of* **kulintang** *musicians, play their gongs at a celebration on Luzon.*

Filipinos have music to suit every occasion. Most large towns and cities have a brass band that plays lively music for holidays and other celebrations, and mournful music for funeral processions. Chanting is an important part of religious ceremonies. Music also plays a part in dating. Sometimes, when a man falls in love with a woman, he sings her a traditional **serenade**, accompanied by a group of musicians called a *rondalla*.

Filipinos also enjoy Spanish guitar songs, as well as classical music and rock 'n' roll. In the late 1960s and early 1970s, Filipinos set their own music and lyrics to a rock beat. Like other kinds of rock music, this style of rock, called Pinoy rock, featured drums, singing, and electric or acoustic guitars.

Gong music

Filipinos continue to play the traditional instruments that their **ancestors** played. The gong, which is believed to have magical qualities, is played at major events, such as weddings and funerals. Gongs are large metal discs that make a ringing note when struck with a hand or stick. The larger the disc, the lower the note the gong produces. Musicians create different sounds with the same gong by changing the way they strike or slide their hand or stick against it.

Gongs range in size from the small *gangsa*, which is flat and played by hand, to the *tagung-guan*, which is so large that musicians hang it from the rafters of a house so they can play it. The *kulintang* is a Maranao instrument made of eight gongs. The gongs are arranged from smallest to largest, and they are played with two long bamboo sticks.

A woman from Mindanao plays a stringed instrument called a **piyapi**, *or "boat lute." The instrument is made from a single log that is hollowed out and carved.*

Musical strings

The Spanish introduced guitars to the Philippines, and they are now an important part of Filipino music. Other stringed instruments are also popular. The *kotyapi* of the Maranao people produces a haunting sound. Each *kotyapi* has a soundbox, shaped a bit like a crocodile, and two strings, which the musician plucks. The Mangyan people on the island of Mindoro play the *git-git*, an instrument like a violin made of animal skin and bark, with strings of long human hair.

Flutes galore

Flutes and pipes are essential to traditional music. Many are made from bamboo. One of the most interesting types of flutes is the nose flute. To play it, a musician puts the flute to his or her nostril and blows gently. Filipinos also play panpipes. A panpipe is actually several pipes that are tied together in a row, from longest to shortest. A musician blows across the top of the panpipe to create an airy sound.

(above) Organists from all over the world travel to Las Piñas to play Diego Cera's bamboo pipe organ.

A bamboo pipe organ

Bamboo is used to make instruments other than flutes and pipes, including drums, **castanets**, and xylophones. The most unusual bamboo instrument is the famous pipe organ in Las Piñas, near Manila. A Roman Catholic **friar** named Diego Cera built the organ in the early 1800s. Cera wanted a metal pipe organ for his church, but it was too expensive. Bamboo was cheap and plentiful in the Philippines, so he decided to build the organ from bamboo. No other organ in the world had been made from the grass, but Cera was sure it would work, and it did.

To play a bamboo flute, a person must purse together his or her lips and blow air across an opening at the top of the flute. Covering different holes along the flute allows a person to play different notes.

Time to dance

Rizal Park, in Manila, is a good place to dance on a sunny day.

Filipinos are famous for their complex and beautiful traditional dances. Professional **troupes** perform these dances for audiences around the world. The dances are also part of many festivals and ceremonies. In addition, Filipinos enjoy forms of dance that began in other countries, such as ballroom and ballet dancing. Young people also like to dance to pop and techno music.

Telling stories

In traditional Filipino dances, the dancers often tell stories with their movements. They act out folktales or myths about ancient gods and heroes. They imitate the movements of daily events, such as planting, harvesting, fishing, and hunting. While preparing for a hunt, certain groups of Filipinos reenact a successful hunt with a dance, to bring themselves good luck.

A member of the Ramon Obuson Folkloric Group performs a dance about the history of the Philippines.

The *tinikling*

The movements of birds inspire many traditional Filipino dances. The *tinikling*, or "dance of the herons," imitates the heron-like tikling bird, which gracefully and speedily walks between tree branches and long grass stems in the wild. During the *tinikling*, men sit on the floor, knocking long bamboo poles together. Female performers quickly step, hop, and twirl between the moving poles while gracefully moving their arms.

The *singkil*

The *singkil* is another famous Filipino dance that involves bamboo poles and requires fast footwork. It tells the story of a princess caught in a stormy forest and the prince who finds her. A woman dressed in a colorful gown plays the princess. She holds two fans and wears the *singkil*, or tinkling ankle bells, after which the dance is named. The princess is accompanied by servants who dance and shield her with a parasol. The storm begins as four men, who play angry monkeys, bang bamboo poles on the floor. The princess and servants must dance between the poles, never touching them. The storm worsens and the bamboo poles move faster, drowning out the tinkling of the *singkil*. The dance ends when the prince frightens away the storm.

*Dancers playing the roles of the prince, princess, and servants practice the **singkil** before a performance.*

The Bayanihan dancers

The Filipinesca Pacifica Dance Company, the Ballet Philippines, and the Bayanihan Philippine Dance Company are some of the Filipino dance troupes that perform around the world. All are a source of national pride, especially the Bayanihan company. Formed in the 1950s, its members devote themselves to preserving their country's most exciting music, costumes, and traditional dances, including spectacular religious dances and folk dances such as the *tinikling*.

Languages past and present

At least 70 languages are spoken today in the Philippines, some by large numbers of Filipinos and others by just a few people living in the countryside. Many languages are related, but that does not mean that people from one place can understand people from another. Isolated from one another by water, mountains, and jungles, almost every Filipino group developed its own words, pronunciations, and expressions over thousands of years.

Official languages

So that people living in different parts of the Philippines could understand one another, the United States declared English the country's official language when it ruled the Philippines during the early 1900s. In 1937, a new Filipino government decided to replace English with a language called Filipino. Filipino is based on Tagalog, the most widely spoken Philippine language. Today, both Filipino and English are the country's official languages.

This child from Cebu looks at a storybook written in English. In school, children from Cebu learn to speak and read in English, Filipino, and Cebuano.

Ancient writing

Long ago, different groups of Filipinos used different alphabets. At least ten alphabets existed throughout the islands! When the Spanish conquered the Philippines, they introduced their alphabet. In the following years, the Spanish banned many of the Filipino alphabets, and most were eventually forgotten. Two peoples still write in their ancient alphabets. The Mangyan, from Mindoro, and the Pala'wan, from the southwestern island of Palawan, use their alphabets to carve love poems and messages on strips of bamboo.

These people in Manila speak both English and Filipino. Filipino has more than three million words — about three times as many as English!

Other languages

Filipinos often use their regional languages in everyday life and when writing works of literature. Some of the most common regional languages in the Philippines are Ilocano and Ilonggo, spoken in northern Luzon; Hiligaynon, spoken mostly in the Visayan Islands, in the center of the country; and Cebuano, also spoken in the Visayan Islands and on Mindanao.

An English-Filipino dictionary

In Filipino, there are two ways to speak to someone — a polite, formal way for speaking with strangers or others to whom one should show respect, and an informal way for addressing friends. You can try speaking informal Filipino with the words in the chart.

English	Filipino
Welcome! or Long life!	*Mabuhay!*
Good morning.	*Magandang umaga.*
Good afternoon.	*Magandang hapon.*
Good evening.	*Magandang gabi.*
How are you?	*Kumusta ka?*
I'm fine.	*Mabuti naman.*
Please.	*Paki* or *Bigyan ng kasiyahan.*
Thank you.	*Salamat.*
You're welcome.	*Walang anuman.*
Yes.	*Oo.*
No.	*Hindi.*
Okay.	*Sige.*
I don't know.	*Hindi ko alam.*
What is your name?	*Anong pangalan mo?*
My name is _____.	*Ako si _____.*

Folklore and literature

Telling folktales and myths is an ancient part of Filipino culture. The oldest tales describe how plants, animals, and other parts of the world came to exist. They include stories about how the carabao got its split hoof from stomping on a turtle, how a pearl necklace formed the stars, and how lizards got their beautiful markings by tattooing one another's backs. Other folktales teach people how to behave by telling about people and animals who were rewarded or punished for their actions. Many later tales, influenced by stories brought from Spain, tell about saints, treasures, kings, and poor men who married princesses.

By word of mouth

Long ago, storytellers who could not read or write memorized Filipino legends and folktales. They recited them while people worked, at night around the fire, or at festivals. Younger people heard the stories, memorized them, and recited them to others. The stories were passed this way from generation to generation. The longest stories that people recited are called epics. Epics are long poems that describe the adventures of ancient heroes, who often have magical powers. Many epics are sung rather than spoken, and are shared in parts over several days.

(top) The Spanish influence on the Philippines can be seen in this illustration from a Filipino book from the 1800s. Characters from a traditional Filipino folktale are dressed in Spanish fashions that were popular at the time.

(opposite) Some Filipino stories tell about families and their everyday lives. This illustration comes from a story about a Filipino family that lived on Catanduanes Island in the 1800s.

Epics

The *Maragtas*, from the Hiligaynon people of the western Visayan Islands, tells the story of the great chiefs who led their people across the sea to settle in the Philippines long ago. The chiefs bought land in their new country from the Ati, and formed a friendship with them that is mentioned in the *Maragtas*. This friendship is celebrated in festivals such as *Ati-Atihan*.

Another epic is the *Hudhud* of the Ifugao. It tells many stories, including one about Bugan, a warrior princess, and Daulayan, the poor man whom she chooses as her husband. A female storyteller sings the *Hudhud* to harvesters to relieve their boredom as they work. As she sings, the workers sing in reply.

(above) A monument honoring the author and Philippine hero Dr. José Rizal was built in Manila. The monument includes a statue of Rizal and a plaque with one of his poems, Mi Ultimo Adios, or "My Complete Goodbye."

Writing and rebellion

Almost all the epics, myths, and other ancient Filipino tales still told today were written down after the Spanish conquered the Philippines. The Spanish brought technology, such as paper-making and printing presses, which allowed Filipinos to copy and store the tales in books. Many modern Filipino authors and poets use these collections of stories as inspiration for their own work.

The struggle of Filipinos throughout history is a major theme of Philippine writing. Dr. José Rizal wrote one of the country's best-known novels in 1886. *Noli me tangere*, or *Touch Me Not*, portrays the many troubles the Philippines faced under Spanish rule. Rizal's writing and leadership caused so many Filipinos to turn against the government that the Spanish eventually killed him.

A tale of the carabao

Filipinos tell several stories about the carabao. The Tagalog, who live mainly on Luzon, tell the following story about how the carabao, one of the largest animals in the country, is tricked by one of the smallest animals, a hummingbird.

How Carabao was fooled

One afternoon, Carabao was lying under a tall, shady narra tree to avoid the hot sun. Hummingbird landed on a branch above him.

"Good day, Carabao," she said cheerily.

"Good day," Carabao replied.

"I'm on my way to the river to get a drink of water," explained Hummingbird. "I get so thirsty in this hot weather that I could drink an entire river!"

"You? Drink an entire river?" Carabao laughed. "You're so tiny that you'd drown if a raindrop fell on you!"

Hummingbird decided to challenge Carabao to a contest. "You'd be surprised how much I can drink!" she said slyly. "Even more than you. Meet me later at the river and I'll prove it."

"There's no way you can drink more than me," Carabao snorted, but he was also intrigued. He accepted the challenge, and met Hummingbird at the river later that afternoon.

Carabao stood ankle-deep in the water as Hummingbird sat above him in a tree. "Now, I'll prove that I can drink much more than you can, little bird," Carabao said as he bent down to drink. He drank quickly at first, then more slowly as his stomach began to fill with water. He drank more than he ever had before! To his surprise, the river began to swell up around his knees. He kept swallowing until he thought his stomach would burst, but the water rose so high that he had to hobble to the shore before he drowned. He collapsed there on his side, so full he could not move.

"You didn't drink a drop!" Hummingbird said accusingly.

"Of course I did!" gasped the baffled Carabao. "I drank enough to fill a lake!"

"Then why is the water higher than it was before?" Hummingbird challenged.

"I ... I don't understand!" Carabao stammered.

They debated for a very long time about whether Carabao drank any water at all. Finally, Hummingbird told Carabao, "It doesn't matter how much you drank. I will drink more water from the river than you could in your life."

Hovering in the air, Hummingbird dipped her tiny beak into the water. It looked as if she were sipping up nearly the entire river! Carabao could not believe his eyes, and lowered his head in defeat.

In fact, Hummingbird was playing a trick on Carabao. She had chosen a place for her challenge that was near the mouth of the river, where tides made the water rise and fall. Carabao drank while the high tide was rolling in. No matter how much he drank, the water level kept going up! When it was Hummingbird's turn to drink after the long debate, the tide was rolling out. Hummingbird had timed her trick perfectly!

Proud of her cunning, Hummingbird just looked at Carabao and said, "You see, Carabao, even though you're larger than I am, I can still drink more than you." With a laugh, she flew off, leaving Carabao by the riverbank, still too heavy with water to move.

Glossary

ancestor A person from whom one is descended

animist A person who believes that there are spirits in nature

artisan A skilled craftsperson

bamboo A long, woody grass with hollow stems

baptize To sprinkle with water or dip in water as a sign of washing away sin, in the Christian religion

castanets A pair of small, hollow disks that are worn on the fingers and clicked together to make music

corruption Dishonesty, often in politics or business

crucify To put to death by nailing to a cross

custom Something that a group of people has done for so long that it becomes an important part of their way of life

denomination A religious group within a faith

fast To stop eating food or certain kinds of food for religious or health reasons

friar A member of a religious group who is not allowed to own property and who makes his living by begging

holy Having special religious importance

lance A long wooden pole with a sharp iron or steel head

mass The main religious ceremony of the Roman Catholic Church

missionary A person who travels to a foreign country to spread a particular religion

papier-mâché Shreds of paper mixed with glue that are molded into shapes, dried, and painted

procession A group of persons or vehicles moving along in an orderly, formal manner

prophet A person who is believed to speak on behalf of God

saint A person recognized by a religious faith as being holy

serenade A romantic love song that one person sings to another

troupe A group of actors, singers, or dancers

 # Index